This is a guitarist.

The guitar strings are strummed or plucked...

a pick

...with fingers or a pick.

Parts of a guitar:

pegs

frets

neck

strings

The strings are pressed
onto the frets.

This is a classical Spanish guitar.

Rock bands have electric guitars.

Guitars can have six strings or four strings.

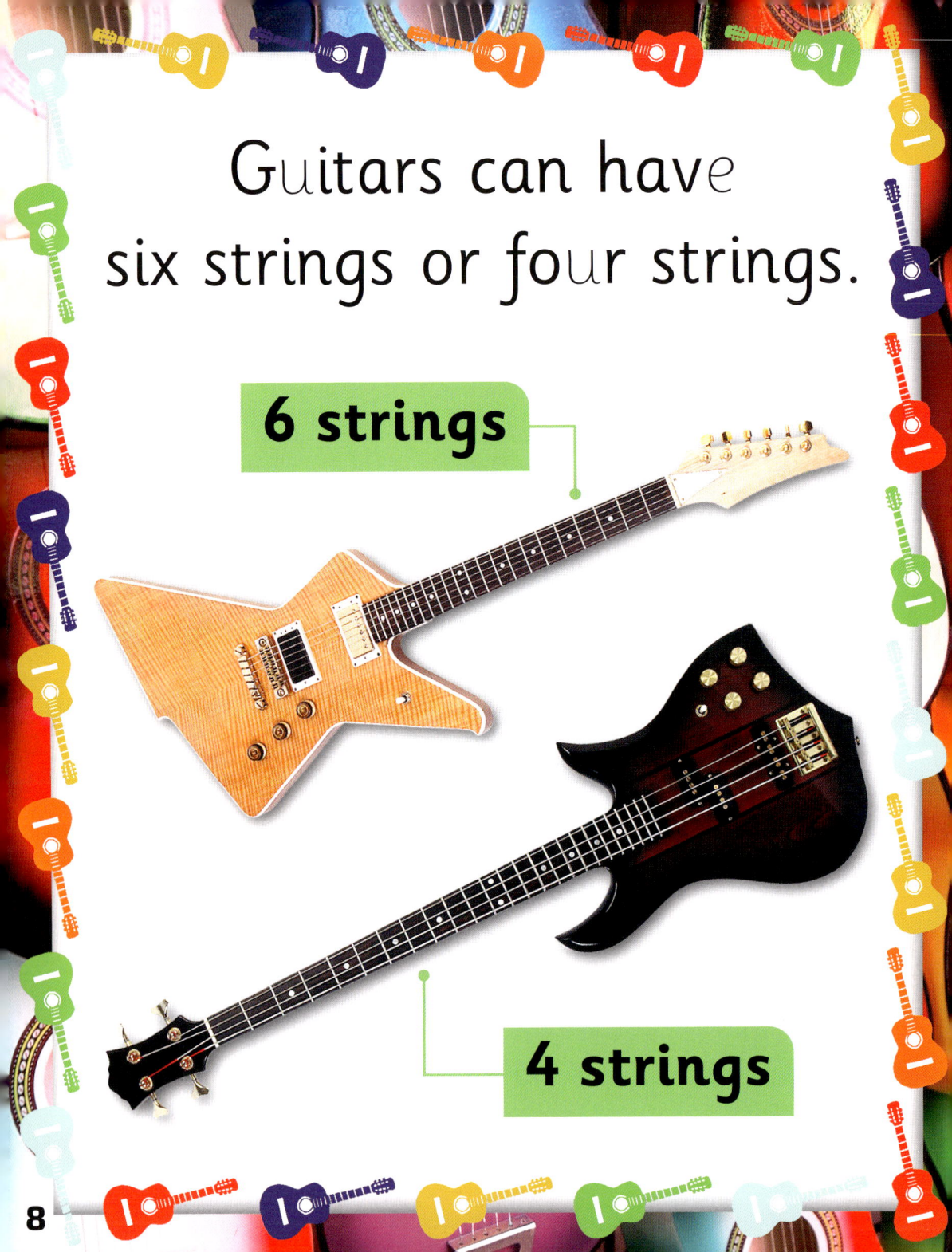

6 strings

4 strings